199/P

Heartfelt ways to say . . .

Good-bye

by
Rhonda Rainey

Sterling Publishing Co., Inc., New York
A Sterling/Chapelle Book

Heartfelt Ways to Say Good-bye

Owner: Jo Packham
Art Design: Rhonda Rainey
Book Design: Linda Orton
Editorial: Ginger Mikkelsen   Images © 1996 Photodisc, Inc.

Library of Congress Cataloging-in-Publication Data

Heartfelt ways to say good-bye / [compiled] by Rhonda Rainey.
      p.   cm.
   "A Sterling/Chapelle Book"
   ISBN 0-8069-0835-1
   1. Farewells--Quotations, maxims, etc.   I. Rainey, Rhonda.
   PN6084.F25H43 1997
   082--dc21
                                                  97-41083
                                                  CIP

10 9 8 7 6 5 4 3 2 1

A Sterling/Chapelle Book
Published by Sterling Publishing Company, Inc.
387 Park Avenue South, New York, NY 10016
© 1998 by Chapelle Ltd.
Distributed in Canada by Sterling Publishing
c/o Canadian Manda Group, One Atlantic Avenue, Suite 105
Toronto, Ontario, Canada M6K 3E7
Distributed in Great Britain and Europe by Cassell PLC
Wellington House, 125 Strand, London WC2R 0BB, England
Distributed in Australia by Capricorn Link (Australia) Pty Ltd.
P.O. Box 6651, Baulkham Hills, Business Centre, NSW 2153, Australia
Printed in Hong Kong
All Rights Reserved

Every effort has been made
to ensure that all of the
information in this book
is accurate.

If you have any questions or
comments please contact:
Chapelle Ltd., Inc.
P.O. Box 9252
Ogden, UT 84409
Phone: (801) 621-2777
FAX: (801) 621-2788

Sterling ISBN 0-8069-0835-1

For Gary,
with love.

1946-1997

Remembrance is the

For love doth guard it,

sweetest flower of all

sun or shower, and friendship

this world perfuming,

keeps it blooming.

— *Clifton Bingham*

Even though
our song has ended,

the melody remains.

Grow not
too high,
grow not
too far
from home.

— Edna St. Vincent Millay

Leonda Finney©

They lived
    and laughed
        and loved
            and left.

— James Joyce

YOU may

deny me to

accompany you,

but you cannot

hinder me

from following.

— Samuel Johnson

I have thought
   of meetings and for
Every meeting a good-by.

I have asked to be left
   a few tears
And some laughter.

— Carl Sandburg

. . .How sweet the road-side flowers might be
If they did not mean good-bye, old friend.

Meng Hao-jan

Good-bye Old Friend

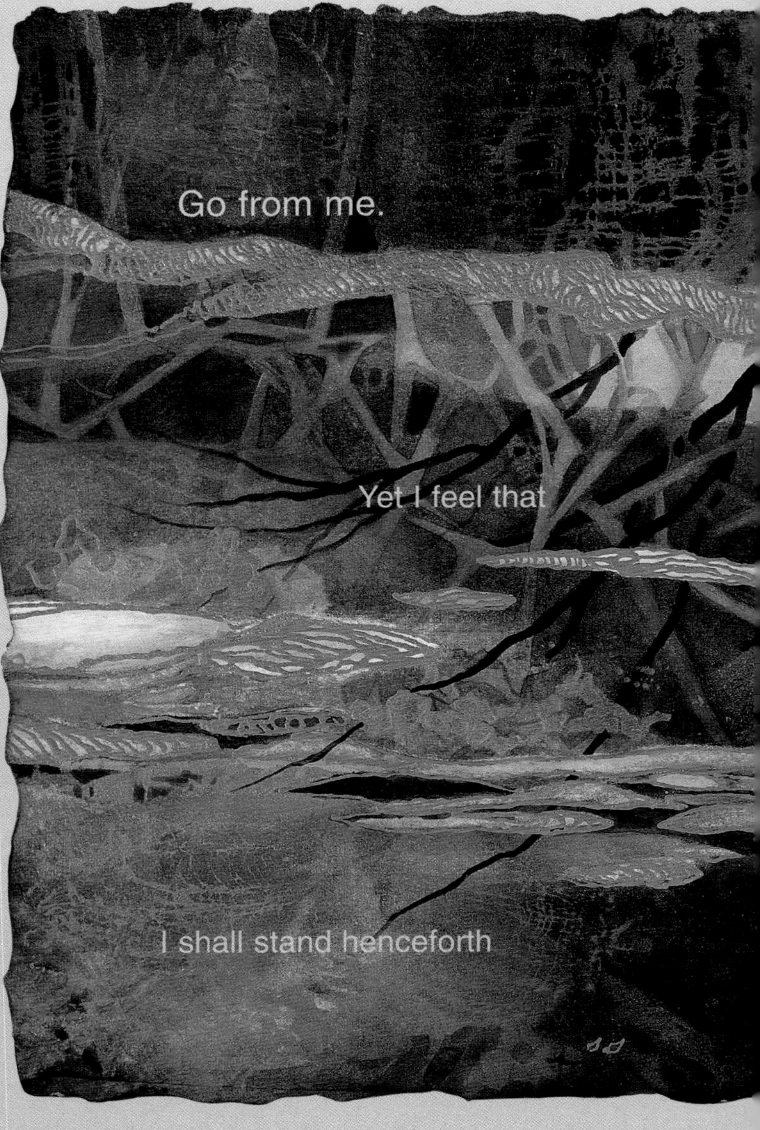

Go from me.

Yet I feel that

I shall stand henceforth

in thy shadow.

Elizabeth Barrett Browning

A brief *parting* from those dear

is the worst ONE has to *fear*.

— Joseph Conrad

Will somebody tell me why people let go?

e.e. cummings

This is the end of the past.
Be happy.

W. S. Merwin

You never really leave a place or a
person you love. Part of them you
take with you, leaving a part of
yourself behind.

Author Unknown

Thinking of you,

and all that was,

and all that might

have been

and
n o w
w i l l
never be.

Christina Rossetti

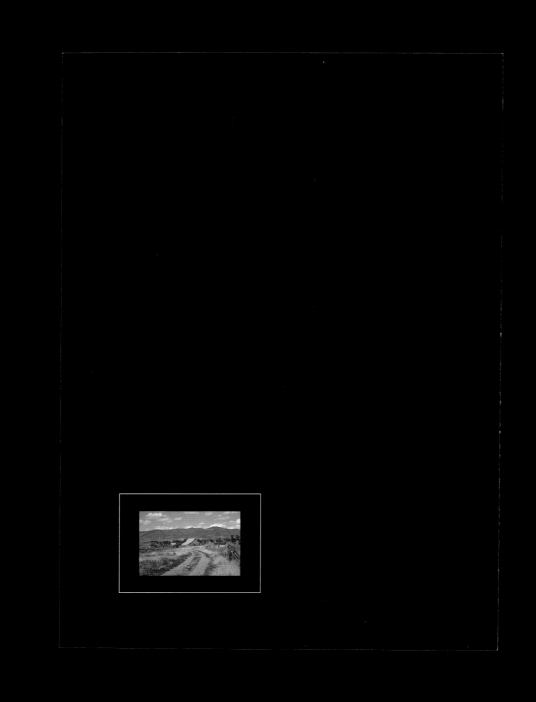

Shake hands, here's luck, good-bye.
But if you come to a road where danger,
or guilt, or anguish, or shame's to share,
Be good to the one that loves you true,
...And whistle and I'll be there.

A.E. Housman

Loosen your hands,

Let go and say good-bye.

Let the stars and songs go.

Let the faces and years go.

Loosen your hands and say good-bye.

— Carl Sanburg

The sunshine of my soul

Is in those eyes,

And when they leave me, all the world is night.

— Lady John Scott

Go where Glory waits thee,

But . . . oh, remember me.

— Thomas Moore

The heart remembers

even

although the mind forgets

and the agonies

the raptures

the hopes

and the regrets

But, something of the
m a g i c
lingers,
never to
d e p a r t ;
d e e p
down in
t h e
s e c r e t
places of
the quiet
h e a r t .

— Patience Strong

Farewell,

Farewell,

be

always

young.

Edna St. Vincent Millay

Adieu

Where'er you tread,
    the blushing flowers will rise,
And all things flourish
    where you turn your eyes.

— Alexander Pope

Thy mind
shall be a
mansion for
all lovely forms,

thy memory be as a dwelling place for all
sweet sounds and memories. . .

With what healing thoughts of tender joy
wilt thou remember me.
— William Wordsworth

I go with my friend,

As far as the river bank.

She is gone –

and my mind is filled

and overflowing

with the things I did not say.

– Liu Shih-an

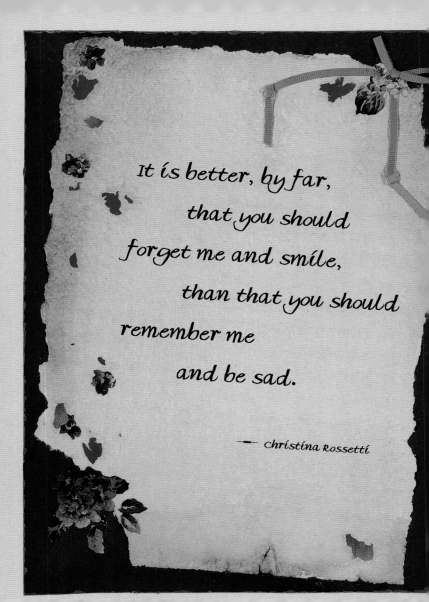

It is better, by far,

that you should

forget me and smile,

than that you should

remember me

and be sad.

— Christina Rossetti

open your heart, i'll give you a treasure, a piece of forever.

e.e. cummings

follow your heart

forget me not

God
knows no distance.

— *Charleszetta Waddles*

Wherever I roam,
Whatever realms to see,
My heart, untraveled,
Fondly turns to thee.

— Oliver Goldsmith

It was a night of early spring,
The winter-sleep was scarcely broken;
Around us shadows and the wind
Listened for what was never spoken.

Though half a score of years are gone,

Spring comes as sharply now as then—

But if we had it all to do

It would be done the same again.

It was a spring that never came;
But we have lived enough to know
That what we never have, remains;
It is the things we have that go.

— Sara Teasdale

Please accept this hand picked willow sapling

And plant it by your bedroom window.

Think of me when it buds after a rainy day.

— *Hong Lang*

When the golden sun is sinking.

And your mind from care is free.

When of others you are thinking.

Will you sometimes think of me?

— *Alice Schenberger*

Good-bye and God bless you,
old friend;
and keep your heart fresh,
and your memory green

**for the old days that
will never come again.**
       Samuel Clemens

Remember me when I am gone away . . .
When you can no more hold me by the hand . . .

— Christina Rossetti

Oh, while I was with you
Then I was clean and brave,
And miles around the wonder grew
How well did I behave.

And now you pass me by,
And nothing will remain,
And miles around they'll say that I
Am quite myself again.

— A. E. Housman

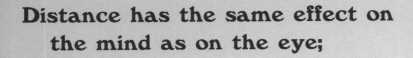

Distance has the same effect on the mind as on the eye;

and while we glide around the stream of
time,
whatever we leave behind us is always
lessening,
and that which we approach
increasing . . .

— **Samuel Johnson**

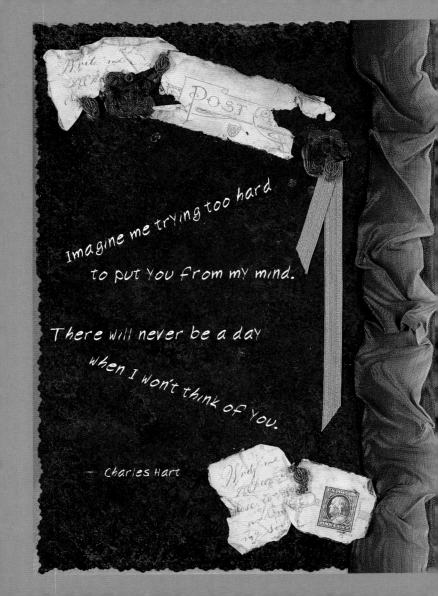

Imagine me trying too hard
to put you from my mind.

There will never be a day
when I won't think of you.

— Charles Hart

If I should be
       where I no more can hear thy voice,
nor catch from thy wild eyes
       these gleams of past existence —
wilt thou then forget.

— William Wordsworth

How shall you
speak of parting?

How shall the
bands be
loosened

that   friendship

fastened around

you?

— Madeline Mason-Manheim

How shall you
speak of parting?

How shall the
bands be
loosened

that   friendship

fastened around

you?

— Madeline Mason-Manheim

With you I leave

a *remembrance* of miracles

— e.e. cummings

There have
been so many
to say good-bye to.
And now, something
inside of me
is about
ready for some
hello's.

— Vicki Crow